TABLE OF CONTENTS

Workbook Answers

Reading: Foundational Skills

Fill in the Blank! (Long Vowels) Answers
1. bone
2. plane
3. kite
4. cane
5. stones

Fill in the Blank! (Short Vowels) answers
1. bed
2. hut
3. shed
4. rat
5. grin

Vowel Teams answers
1. c - braid
2. d - law
3. d - breathe
4. b - height
5. a - rope
6. b - soil
7. d- steak
8. d -put
9. c - tied
10. c - proud

What Word Is Missing? Answers
1. remote
2. entire

3. explode
4. pancakes
5. flagpole
6. include
7. inside
8. athlete
9. invites
10. snowflakes

Understanding Words with Prefixes and Suffixes answers
1. connects to loudest
2. connects to unhappy
3. connects to rewrite
4. connects to builder
5. connects to happiest
6. connects to winner
7. connects to quickly
8. connects to unpack
9. connects to stacked
10. connects to younger

A Letter to Grandma and Grandpa answers
1. How
2. write
3. busy
4. Ocean
5. been
6. heard
7. brought
8. enough
9. crowded
10. people

Language

Collective Nouns answers
1. team
2. swarm
3. band
4. class
5. audience
6. family
7. crowd
8. herd
9. flock
10. group

Irregular Plural Nouns answers
1. sheep
2. people
3. feet
4. children
5. moose
6. men
7. fish
8. teeth
9. elves
10. babies

Reflexive Pronouns answers
1. yourself
2. herself
3. themselves
4. himself
5. itself
6. myself
7. yourselves

8. ourselves

Past Tense Irregular Verbs answers
1. ran
2. was
3. brought
4. began
5. chose
6. came
7. flew
8. froze
9. made
10. broke

Adjectives answers
1. spicy
2. sweet
3 feminine
4. beautiful
5. delicious
6. lots
7. loud
8. Active
9. Outstanding
10. foreign

Adverbs answers
1. fast
2. politely
3. really
4. never
5. ferociously
6. softly

7. gently
8. always
9. angrily
10. carefully

A for Adjective, B for Adverb answers

1. a
2. b
3. a
4. a
5. b
6. b
7. a
8. b
9. b
10. b

Sense and Nonsense answers

1. I helped my mother cook supper.
2. The dog is chewing on a bone.
3. The fire truck went past my house.
4. Horses are beautiful animals.
5. Dad made us sandwiches for lunch.
6. Mr. Smith is our new teacher.
7. Hang the painting above the couch.
8. Our cat has three kittens.
9. That is a pretty dress.
10. We will wash the car this weekend.

Compound Sentences answers

1. Joe likes hot dogs, and I like hamburgers.
2. Yesterday it rained, but today it's sunny.

3. We can play tag, or we can jump rope.
4. Mom was on the phone, so I talked softly to the baby.
5. I like reading books, and I like flying kites.

Capitalization answers
1. James said his family is going to Disney World in August.
2. This Christmas, Grandma Smith is coming to visit.
3. My birthday is on September 17th.
4. I kissed Mom and Dad goodnight.
5. Have you ever been to Atlanta, Georgia?
6. Thanksgiving always falls on the 4th Thursday of November.
7. Here is my assignment, Mr. Jones.
8. My big sister goes to the University of Texas.
9. At church, Reverend Brown told us about Noah's ark.
10. My uncle's car is a Nissan Sentra.

Commas in Letter Writing answers
1. Dear Mom and Dad,
2. Dear Sir or Madam,
3. Sincerely, Bonnie Smith
4. Love, Caitlin
5. Your friend, Billy

Apostrophes answers
1. Fred's
2. it's
3. we'll
4. can't
5. don't
6. parents'
7. cat's
8. school's
9. sister's

10. Jones'

General Spelling Patterns answers
1. height
2. night
3. boy
4. boil
5. blow
6. clown
7. badge
8. cage
9. light
10. write

Formal and Informal English answers
1. I
2. I
3. F
4. F
5. F
6. I
7. I
8. I
9. F
10. F

Using Context to Understand New Words answers
1. d - sad
2. a - tasty
3. b - confused
4. b - mess
5. c - hardly

Using Prefixes to Understand Words answers
1 connects to pre-game
2 connects to disappear
3 connects to disprove
4 connects to disability
5 connects to rebuild
6 connects to unbelievable
7 connects to bimonthly
8 connects to impolite
9 connects to bicycle
10 connects to misunderstand

Using Root Words to Understand New Words answers
1. friend
2. tall
3. sleep
4. run
5. talk
6. loud
7. crown
8. teach
9. book
10. bore

Combine Words to Make Compound Words answers
1. football
2. classroom
3. downpour
4. cheeseburger
5. doorknob
6. butterfly
7. treehouse
8. windowsill
9. fireplace
10. policeman

Related Words answers

1. snow   sleds   icicles
These all have to do with winter.

2. fire   sun   heater
There are all hot things

3. hat   shirt   gloves
These are all things a person wears

4. red   yellow   blue
These are all colors

5. small   medium   large
These are all sizes

6. kitten   puppy   calf
These are all young animals

7. cherry   pear   peach
These are all fruits

8. oven   toaster   blender
These are all things found in a kitchen

9. uncle   aunt   grandmother
These are all relatives

10. book   newspaper   magazine
These are all things people read

.

Reading: Literature

Bookstore Passage answers
1. d – Books Are Not Boring
2. d – not enough information
3. a - Saturday
4. b – they were about food
5. café
6. foreign
7. c - Europe
8. b - Japan

The Elephant's Child answers
1. C: Fables and fairy tales often start out with the phrase "once upon a time", and true stories usually don't.

2. A: A fable is a story that isn't true, but teaches a lesson. It's a lot like a fairy tale.

3. D: The main idea of the story is how the elephant got his trunk, so that would be a good title.

4. C: He wanted the baby elephant to get closer so he could eat him.

5. D: Even though a crocodile almost ate him, the baby elephant wound up with a new trunk that was much better than his old nose, and it was because he was curious.

Benjamin Franklin Passage answers
1. b - 1706
2. c – the family was poor
3. a – desire to know and learn
4. c – Founding Fathers
5. c – being a talk show host

6. a – Great Britain
7. b – The Life of Benjamin Franklin
8. d – cost a lot of money
9. a – Boston, Massachusetts
10. d – Benjamin Franklin was one of the greatest Americans ever

Babe Zaharias passage answers
1. b – a person who is one of the first to do something
2. a – the story of someone's life
3. b – Port Arthur, Texas
4. c – 48
5. d – basketball
6. c – Babe Zaharias: One of the World's Greatest Athletes
7. d – to be very good at something
8. a – golf
9. d – Beaumont, Texas
10. b – 1911

Johnny Appleseed answers
1. so Ruth can learn about Johnny Appleseed
2. applesauce
3. the first sentence tells us she's eating applesauce and it's her favorite dessert
4. a – popular   b – silently   c – legend
5. plant

Becoming a Doctor answers
1. c - 20
2. a – graduate   b – respected   c – prepared
3. they are medical school graduates training in hospitals
4. Becoming
5. all answers are valid

A Trip to a Farm answers

1. boring
2. to show that someone is speaking those words
3. she meant he would change his mind (or that he would have fun)
4. a – corn   b – apple   c – watermelon
5. milking a cow and riding a pony

Penguins answers

1. over ten thousand
2. don't
3. unusual
4. 10,000
5. they are too heavy and their wings are too stiff

The Giraffe answers

1. 20
2. b – to share information with us
3. badly fully pounds tallest
4. any three of: leaves, twigs, grass, fruit, shrubs
5. fighting

Thomas Edison: The Man Who Changed the World answers

1. Little Thomas Edison | Mr. Inventor | He Changed the World
2. Little Thomas Edison
3. answers will be different, but should reflect material in the text
4. plant, plus, bed, man
5. because he got kicked out of school

The State Fair of Texas answers

1. state   goats   three   shows
2. the Texas Star
3. no

- 15 -

4. He is 52 feet tall
5. personal; no correct answer

Practice Test #1 Answers

Answers and Explanations

1. D: Christmas.
The names of holidays need to be capitalized. Choice A is not capitalized. The other choices are spelled wrong.

2. B: Anna's.
"Anna's" shows that the house belongs to one person, Anna. The other choices are incorrect. Choice A is not capitalized, Choice C does not have an apostrophe, and Choice D uses two words that do not correctly complete the sentence.

3. A: Your friend,
Letters need a closing. The closing has a comma at the end of a phrase, followed by the name of the person who wrote the letter. The other choices do not use commas. Choice B has a period at the end. Periods are for the ends of sentences. Choice C has a semicolon at the end. Semicolons are usually used to connect two related sentences together. Choice D has no punctuation at all.

4. D: The fish
The magic fish gave Yeh-shen one wish. She wished to be able to go to the king's party.

5. A: She was very unhappy.
Yeh-shen's stepmother was mad. She said that Yeh-shen was too poor to put on the slipper.

6. B: A long time ago in the countryside of China
The beginning of the story says that it happened a long time ago in China, but it doesn't exactly say where. However, Yeh-shen lives by a river and talks to many animals. That makes it likely that she lived in the countryside. She would not see many animals if she lived in a big city.

- 17 -

7. D: The story of Cinderella

Yeh-shen is sometimes called the Chinese Cinderella. The stories are very similar. Cinderella and Yeh-shen both live with their stepmothers and stepsisters. They both have to work hard. They are able to go to a special party because of a magical wish. They both lose their slippers and marry the ruler of the land.

8. C: It is good to be kind.

Yeh-shen was kind to everyone, even her stepmother and stepsisters. Her kindness helped her live happily, even when she was very poor and had to work hard.

9. C: She was poor but gave him some of her food.

Yeh-shen was kind to everyone, even the fish. Yeh-shen was very poor, so she had little food for herself. Still she saved some of her food for the fish.

10. A: Did they go to the palace, too?

After Yeh-shen marries the king, the story ends. The narrator does not tell us what happened to Yeh-shen's selfish stepmother or stepsisters. This question asks about what happened to them after Yeh-shen got married.

11. C: group

Mary saw a lot of people at the park, so the right noun here is "group."

12. B: children

The noun needs to match the verb in the sentence. The question is about how many, so the noun that follows needs to be a plural noun. The other choices are all singular.

13. D: ourselves

"We" is the subject of the sentence, so the reflexive pronoun that fits in the blank is "ourselves."

14. C: sat

The sentence mentions something that happened "yesterday." That means the correct form of this irregular verb is in the simple past tense. The other verbs are not in the correct tense.

15. A: new

Choice A is the only adjective (describing word) in this list.

16. D: Josh ate the whole box of cereal.

This is the only correct choice. The sentence needs to be in the past tense and is about a boy who ate a box of cereal. Choice A is missing the main idea (that Josh ate the cereal), Choice B is in the present tense, and Choice C mixes up the subject (Josh) and object (the box of cereal).

17. D: What kind of frog is this, Mrs. Smith?

This is the best choice because it uses a polite question to ask about frogs. Choice A is informal and could be used with anyone, Choice B is a statement, and Choice C does not include frogs or polite language.

18. A: Bothered

This is the only choice that fits the sentence. The context of the sentence tells us that the boys were bad and that the dog ran away from them. Choices B and D are nice words, so they do not fit into the sentence. Choice C does not make sense, since the "pestering" was something that kept happening until the dog ran away.

19. C: Not usual

The prefix "un" means "not," so the word would mean something NOT common or NOT ordinary. The other choices are not good synonyms for uncommon.

20. C: To make longer

The root word "length" is about distance, or the space between two points. Therefore, the word "lengthen" has to do with distance, or making things longer.

21. B: A thing that keeps the place in a book

This is a compound word that is created from two words to make a new one. A bookmark keeps your place in your book—it shows you information about where you were reading. The other choices do not match the meanings of the two words.

22. D: A hard covering for an arm or leg

This is the only choice that matches the meaning of the word in the sentence. The sentence is about a child having something on after suffering a fracture (broken bone).

23. A: An apple

A juicy food has a lot of water, just like an apple. The other choices are all foods that are dry and do not have much water in them.

24. A: Brave

Since the sentences say Bob is a hero, the word for the blank needs to be a positive one. The other words have similar meanings to "brave," but they are negative in connotation.

25. C: Candles

The paragraph says that people who had no electricity used candles for light.

26. A: Electricity makes life easier.

The paragraph describes how electricity makes our lives easier. We just turn on a lamp for light or open the refrigerator for cold food. However, people did not always have electricity. Choices C and D are related to the details in the paragraph. Choice B is completely wrong.

27. C: Raise your hand and wait to be called on.

The best way to answer a question is to raise your hand and wait until the teacher calls your name. This is a respectful way to be a part of a large group discussion.

28. A: Christmas is celebrated in many countries. But it is not celebrated in all countries. There are many different kinds of people in the United States. In the United States, many people celebrate Christmas, much as they do in Germany.

This is the best choice because it uses the other children's ideas. It builds on those ideas and adds on new information. This is the correct way to add to a group discussion. Choice B builds on Michael's ideas but not Susie's. Choice C does not discuss that Christmas is celebrated in the United States. Choice D is very informative about how Christmas is celebrated in Germany and the United States, but it ignores Michael's comment.

29. B: Why plants are important
The paragraphs talk about the different ways that plants are important. While being a part of an ecosystem and being a kind of food are important, they are not the main ideas. The passage does not talk directly about the reasons for why plants exist.

30. D: Animals eat plants to live, and then they die, making the ground good for plants to grow.
While the other choices are all true, they do not answer the question. The question is about the relationship or connection between plants as something to eat and what happens in an ecosystem.

31. C: Small parts of the ground the plant uses as food
"Mineral" is a common second-grade vocabulary word. Minerals are small parts of the soil that the plant uses to stay healthy.

32. D: Plants and Ecosystems
The relationship between plants and bugs is talked about in the section on ecosystems. The other choices do not discuss that bugs need to live in or on plants.

33. A: We need plants to live, eat, and breathe.
While all of the other choices are important, they are not the main point of this passage. This passage is an informative passage telling about the importance of plants.

34. B: Plants clean the air and make oxygen.
While all of the choices are true, the question is only asking about a reason why people need plants to breathe.

35. B: Frogs eat bugs and flies.
This sentence is the best way to put the sentences together. The sentences needed to be revised into one sentence with a single topic (what frogs eat). The other choices do not include all of the information.

36. D: Ask your teacher to help you find websites for your report. Each student reads a different website. Then the group gets together to write the report. Ask the teacher to look at the report before you put it on the classroom's homepage.

This choice is the best answer because it shows that you worked together as a team, got assistance from your teacher in doing research, wrote the report as a team, and then had the teacher check your work before you posted it on the homepage. Choice A does not include using guidance from your teacher, Choice B does not include using the computer to help with developing the report, and Choice C does not involve teamwork.

37. B: We first planted the bean in some dirt (Day 1). We watered the bean, and it started to grow (Day 7). The bean plant later grew some leaves (Day 21). Finally, the bean plant grew tall (Day 30).
This is the best choice, because it uses the work from the group, then it adds in some information. It is also in paragraph form. Choice A is not complete; it is missing important information and does not have the concluding information. Choice C does not put the information into a paragraph. Choice D is not written as a science report.

38. A: White, high

The two-syllable word "firefly" has two long "i" sounds in it. "White" and "high" both have long "i" sounds. Choice B has a long "i" sound (fly) and short "i" sound (pitch). Choice C has a long "i" sound (tire) and short "i" sound (skip). Choice D has a short "i" sound (list) and a long "i" sound (why).

39. B: Teacher

The suffix "-er" makes the word mean "a doer" of something. So a "teach<u>er</u>" is a person who teaches. Choice A is a verb in the simple present. Choice C means to teach again, another verb. Choice D is in the past tense.

40. C: Eye, hand

The word "island" is an irregularly spelled word. The "s" is not heard, and the "i" is long.

Practice Test #2 Answers

Answers and Explanations

1. B: My favorite food is pizza. It is really tasty, because it has a lot of vegetables and cheese on it. Pizza is also fun to eat. You don't need to use a fork, knife, or spoon—just your hands! I like to eat pizza with my family. This is the best answer, because it provides two reasons why Min likes pizza and adds in other details. It incorporates prior knowledge about the subject, as well as information on toppings like vegetables and cheese.

2. A: My favorite character is Aslan, the lion. Aslan is the ruler of Narnia, a magical kingdom. He is brave and good. Aslan finds out that the evil White Witch wants to kill Edmund, a boy who hurt his family. Aslan talks to the White Witch and makes a deal. He goes to the camp of the White Witch and takes the place of the Edmund. This shows that Aslan was brave, because he went to the camp alone. It also shows he is good, because he took the place of Edmund. Aslan is an important part of the story, since he stops the White Witch. This is the best answer, because it talks about Fred's opinion, gives support for the opinion, and provides a conclusion. The sentences use linking words appropriately. Choices B and C talk about other story events, not just Fred's favorite character. Choice D also talks about other parts of the story and does not state which character was Fred's favorite.

3. D: It is not hard to make new friends. First, don't be scared! Everyone wants to have a friend. Second, smile at people. A smile is friendly and makes people feel good. Finally, introduce yourself to other people. Tell people your name and then ask them about theirs. Ask about what they like. Soon you will have many new friends! This is the best choice because it has a topic sentence, then three steps with details and, finally, a concluding sentence. Choice A does not have a good opening and closing. Choice B is closer, but it does not offer three steps with details in the middle. Choice C offers advice for looking friendly, but it never mentions the active step toward making friends—introducing yourself—and does not have a solid conclusion.

4. D: I looked at the empty box of donuts on the table. This was the third time someone had stolen donuts from my parent's bakery. I was angry and confused. Who was doing it? First, I looked around the table for clues. Then I saw it. There was a trail of crumbs going out the door! I followed the trail out the door and into the alley. There I found the donut thief: our dog, Rolf! He was munching on the last of the chocolate donuts. I petted him and took him by the collar. "Mom! Dad! I solved the mystery of the missing donuts!"

This paragraph is the best choice. It has a beginning, middle, and end. This story provides details about the mystery (the thefts had happened before, and there were chocolate donuts). It also talks about the storyteller's feelings (I was angry and confused) and has a satisfactory conclusion that gives the reader a feeling of closure.

5. B: 7, 7, 7, 7 The rhyme "Twinkle, Twinkle Little Star" has seven syllables in each line, making the rhyming pattern very easy to remember. This supplies a steady rhythm to the entire poem.

6. D: The beginning tells the problem in the story. The middle gives the action in the story. The ending tells how the characters fixed the problem. Each story contains a beginning, which talks about the characters and the problem which needs to be solved; a middle, which talks about the action and details in the story; and the ending, which shows how the characters solved the problem and how they changed in the story. The other choices all have these different parts out of order.

7. B: Ben feels sorry that his team did not win but will play soccer next year. Although Jenny feels great about the game, Ben's point of view is very different. His team did not win the game, so he probably feels a little unhappy. However, Ben says that his team will try harder next year, showing that he still wants to play soccer.

8. C: A long time ago, a father and mother were very sad. They sat by the fire and talked about their problems. They wanted to keep their troubles secret, but their son hid nearby. He heard it all. This choice best describes what is happening in the illustration. Choice A gives too much information that cannot be seen in the picture. Choice B is about the animals in the picture, but it doesn't mention the woman or the little boy. Choice D does not describe the house in the picture and instead includes a golden coin.

9. D: slowly The verb "walked" is being modified. The only word in the choices that is an adverb, or verb modifier, is "slowly." The other choices are adjectives.

10. B: hid The sentence shows that the initial action is occurring in the simple past tense. The verbs in each part of the compound sentence should be in the same tense. The only choice in the simple past tense is "hid."

11. A: flock A group of birds is referred to as a flock. Choices B and C do not refer to groups, and Choice D refers to a group of horses or cattle.

12. A: What makes Earth like a giant magnet? In this question, you need to find out what makes Earth a magnet, which is Choice A. Choice B is about magnets in general, Choice C is about the reference for the fact, and Choice D is a history question. None of these choices can help you learn more about Earth's magnetism.

13. A: This is the best choice, because it shows what is happening in the story. Choice B is not correct because, although the story mentions that the farmer is sad that he does not have a big family, it does not show what the story is about. Choices C and Choice D are not correct, because they show the pig being sad or angry.

14. D: Sue: "The white cat was on a long branch. Three children were trying to get it to come down. A teacher came with a ladder. She climbed into the tree and rescued the cat." While all of the choices include some details, Choice D is the only one that provides a clear story with the important facts and details in it. Choice A talks too much about how Dale feels about cats,

Choice B does not have enough detail, and Choice C gives a lot of detail about the house, not the incident.

15. C: The little green frog did not say "ribbit-ribbit" but instead said "tibbit-tibbit." This is the only answer that responds with a complete sentence and answers the teacher's question. Choice A does not include a complete sentence. Choice B does not answer the question. Choice D has complete sentences but does not answer the question.

16. A: Ant Chance, a common second-grade vocabulary word, has the short "a" sound, as in the word "ant." Blame, ace, and base all have the long "a" sound.

17. D: Grade The vowel team "ai" can sound like long "a," as it does in this case. Choice D is the only word with the long "a" sound. Choice A has a short "i" sound, Choice B has a long "i" sound, and Choice C has a short "a" sound.

18. A: Bite The uncommon spelling in "light" matches the middle and ending sounds that have a long "i" and a "t." Choice B has a short "i" and "t" sound, Choice C has a short "i" and "t" sound, and Choice D has a short "e" sound and "nt" sound.

19. B: You "Useful" is a common two-syllable vocabulary word. The first "u" is a long vowel. Only Choice B sounds like long "u." Choices A and D have a short "u" sound, and Choice C has an "oy" sound.

20. C: They drank water. Immediately after the boys saw the monkeys, they stopped to get some water. The other choices all came after this event.

21. D: It has an effect on the weather. While all of the other choices provide some facts about the water cycle, they don't answer the question, which is about why the water cycle is significant.

22. B: How the water cycle works and why it is needed. These paragraphs are about the way the cycle works and its importance in everyday life. The other choices only supply important details from the cycle.

23. A: Water vapor An important part of the water cycle is driven by the water droplets in the air.

24. C: To teach how the water cycle works. This is the best choice, because it identifies the purpose in telling the information. Choice A is about the weather, Choice B is about the effects of weather on the cycle, and Choice D is completely wrong in that it mentions that the water cycle changes.

25. B: Little droplets of water in the air. This vocabulary term can be determined from reading the context clues around it or from earlier science lessons.

26. B: Water droplets go into the sky and make clouds. Both reading passages talk about how clouds are formed. Choice A is only from the first reading passage. Choice C is only from the second reading passage. Choice D is true, but it is not an important idea.

27. C: A big pile of paper was put on the table. It was held in place by a bar. This bar (Part A) could move up and down and cut the paper, because it is connected to a wheel. The question asks about how the old-fashioned machine cuts paper. Choice C best describes what the machine in the picture looks like and how it seems to operate. The other options describe something about the machine but not how it would cut paper. Choice A would involve having the papers spin, not be cut. Choice B only describes what the machine looks like and does not mention anything about cutting paper. Choice D only tells that the machine cuts paper, but not how, and then moves on to safety.

28. D: Boil This is a second grade spelling pattern that can be used to write other words.

29. D: Chief According to the dictionary entries here, the word "chef" is incorrect. It should be "chief."

30. A: Excuse me. May I get by? This is an example of formal language. The other choices are informal or even rude language and not appropriate for speaking to adults.

31. A: Don't give up. The prince struggled to reach the princess and save her from the magic spell. Even though he had a difficult time, he kept trying. The other choices do not talk about the prince's struggle or a positive message.

32. C: teeth The correct plural of tooth is teeth. This is a common second grade vocabulary word. Choices B and D are not real words and Choice A is singular.

33. D: himself
William is a boy, and the reflexive pronoun for a boy is "himself." Choice A is for several people (us), B is for you, and C is not a reflexive pronoun.

34. C: Jenny practiced the violin for four hours. Choice C is the only option that makes sense and is grammatically correct.

35. D: Presents All names of people, holidays, products, and places need to be capitalized. So Choice A, B, and C are correctly capitalized. The names of common nouns (Choice D) are not capitalized.

36. A: 1 All greetings in letters need to have a comma (Dear Bob,). Choices B and C already contain commas in the proper places. Choice D is not correct, since Choice A *does* need a comma.

37. C: Didn't The apostrophe stands in for the letter or letters being left out. So the correct form of the contraction is "didn't."

38. D: Melt When you put sugar into water, it becomes part of the water (a solution). You can't see it anymore, but you can still taste it. The sugar does

- 29 -

not "go away" (Choice A) or "explode" (Choice B). Choice C, "appear," has a meaning opposite to that of dissolve.

39. C: Milk Milk is not a spicy food. All of the other foods taste "hot" on your tongue.

40. B: To make again after it has been taken apart. Putting the prefix "re" makes the word mean to "do again," so "rebuild" means "to build again or make something again after it has been destroyed or taken apart."

Additional Bonus Material

Due to our efforts to try to keep this book to a manageable length, we've created a link that will give you access to all of your additional bonus material.

Please visit http://www.mometrix.com/bonus948/terrag2rlwb to access the information.